# When
# Caterpillars Fly

# When Caterpillars Fly

Written by Lisa Mallins

Illustrated by Steve Simpson

Published by Lisa Mallins

Date of publication April 2004

Published by Lisa Mallins, Christopher's, Old Portsmouth Road,
Artington, Guildford, Surrey GU3 1LP

Printed and bound in Great Britain by Knaphill Print,
16 Lower Guildford Road, Knaphill, Surrey GU21 2EG

ISBN 0-9547267-0-7

Picture by Ella aged 9

# Contents

# Inspiration Captured at Last

I am sure that all of us through our paid careers but more importantly through our life career meet a few very talented people that add inspiration to our lives.

As I have progressed through life, I too have developed a more enlightened appreciation of those people with rare talents for whom I have learnt I hope, to take what they have to offer to make my life more purposeful.

This wonderful collection of deeply moving poems and prose started life many years ago as Lisa was growing up, her thoughts now being recorded as she came to work directly with families that are all sharing the one thing that we all fear - the knowledge that our child will not reach adulthood.

Many are funny, many a direct result of sharing experiences, and many a vision to hold in the darkest of times. These offerings are for all of us connected in any way with families who have a child or teenager that has died as a youngster or who will die. Take these in small doses they will cause you to reflect deeply, to remember happy and sad times and often help you to focus on that very special someone.

This book is a tribute to those inspirational families who have faced the darkest of times, have taken courage and made each day count rather than counting every day, Lisa too through this work has shared her inspirational quality with us.

Lisa has chosen that in finally publishing her individual work she will also help one of the few dedicated charities that care for and support these children, young people and their families throughout their very individual journeys, at the beginning, through the highs and lows and after the child has died for however long the family need that support. The charity CHASE Children's Hospice Service is one of just 30 children's hospices in the UK that do just that.

With thanks

Bridget Turner
Director of Care
CHASE Children's Hospice Service

Picture by Rory aged 10

# Introduction

Have you ever started the day, worrying that you haven't got enough milk for your cereal, that you might be late for work because of some slow coach in front of you? Have you ever got so cross at another driver because he didn't move straight away when the traffic lights turned green, felt miserable and annoyed at the world because it was raining, that your hair would get messed up by the wind and get cross and angry because the computers at work aren't working like they should be? Because, of course, a day wouldn't be complete without the odd moan, a good worry and a slight gossip about someone.  Well the families that I wrote this book for have more in their lives than some of us will ever know.  They start their day, every day, with the knowledge that their child may not reach adulthood. And for many this has now turned to reality.

I could never say that I know how these families feel, because I don't. And I could never say that I could take away the pain that they feel, because I can't.  But I can do my best to try and make a slight difference in their lives at some point in their journey.

"When Caterpillars Fly" was written for all of these families, for mums, for dads, grandparents, brothers and sisters, aunts and uncles, friends and relatives, and is in loving memory of their remarkable children who have died with such courage and dignity. I started writing these poems 6 months after I began working for CHASE Children's Hospice Service in Guildford in Surrey as a member of the care team and I wanted this book to be for everyone and anyone.

Our love for our children begins long before they are even born and carries on throughout their life, we expect them to grow, to go to school, to be a teenager, to run around, to eat and drink, to draw, to paint, to grow up to be normal healthy thriving young people, ready to bring up their own children. We all have our dreams of a normal family life. But have we ever considered what happens when things don't go to plan, when you outlive your child and your whole world is turned upside down.  For many families, coping with grief is something they do on a daily basis.

Spend any amount of time with these families and they will show you how to turn a negative into a positive, how to find the good things out of the bad things that are happening to them, and to use their courage and strength to get through the great amount of sadness that life brings for them. Some will tell you how the months or years of struggling to look after a life limited child has been the best months or years of their life and that the little time that they have been able to enjoy together has brought them so much joy and love. Others will tell you how they struggled so hard to watch their child go through so much, and that this part of their lives has been a life changing experience for them and others around them.

I invite you to share some thoughts and learn from their inspiration.

If you ARE one of these families, I thank you for everything you have given to me, and to others, with the hope that this book will be a tribute to you and your children, and to many families in the future. May the caterpillars that have already decided to fly, have peace and love within their world.

Picture by Jamie aged 8

# Dedication

My dedication to this book goes to without doubt, the children, young people and families who have shared their journeys with us. It is in loving memory of their remarkable children who died with such courage, yet in their short lives, despite everything, used their very unique ability, to drain every bit of happiness out of each moment that they had been given, and pass it onto others around them. We all die; but some sooner than others, I wish them peace and serenity in their new world.

Chapter One

# CHASE
# and
# "Christopher's"

"Christopher's"

# CHASE and "Christopher's"

CHASE is a very special and unique children's hospice service that is dedicated to the support of children who are not expected to reach their 19th birthday.

CHASE began in 1994 as a registered charity. They support these remarkable families through their own very individual journeys. This care and support may begin immediately after their child has been diagnosed, throughout the child's life, and beyond, for however long this support is needed.

The CHASE community team visits families in their own home, bringing them emotional support and practical care in a holistic way. "Christopher's" is CHASE's purpose built hospice situated in Artington near Guildford in Surrey. Such a bright, welcoming and happy place, it offers support for all the children and families. There are 9 children's bedrooms in total, all with different themed names and care continues after the child has died with two dedicated bedrooms where the young person can lay at rest. This gives families a chance to say goodbye in their own time, and in their own way. Families can come and stay at "Christopher's" for emotional and practical support, end of life care, or just some well earned respite and are able to stay as a whole family if they choose with family flats for parents, friends and siblings. "Christopher's" also has many fun and relaxing facilities such as a hydrotherapy pool, sensory room, soft play area, teenagers den and much more.

The care team at "Christopher's" and in the community work alongside each other and are committed in giving individualised support to these families. "Christopher's" is a warm, friendly, caring, home from home environment, helping families to enjoy and cherish their time together, however long or short that may be.

The search for a suitable site for a hospice began in 1995. It was long and frustrating. Over a period of nearly two years, about thirty sites were considered, none of which were really suitable. Then in January 1997, the More-Molyneux family, owners of Loseley Park estate in Surrey, offered a piece of land at Artington, just south of Guildford. It seemed to meet all the basic needs and CHASE gratefully accepted the offer.

Planning permission to build had yet to be obtained from local and regional authorities, but the major problem was solved. Among all the many things which now had to be done was the choice of a name. CHASE approached Michael and Sarah More-Molyneux to ask if it could be called "Christopher's", after their son who had been killed in a tragic accident on the estate during that summer. It was a request which both of them found deeply touching and uplifting, and it was willingly granted.

Perhaps even more emotional for them was the day in July 2000, when the first piece of turf was cut at Artington, and when they were invited to raise the CHASE flag; after three years of planning and imagining and talking about it, here now was the start of a building named after their son. They recalled that, when the architect's drawings had first been laid out on the kitchen table at Loseley Park, eleven-year-old Christopher had joined the family, poring over the detailed plans.

And when the hospice welcomed its first families in November 2001, Michael and Sarah were there to celebrate the occasion, to share the sense of achievement, and to applaud the support and contributions of so many hundreds of people.

On the wall of the corridor, just inside the front hall of "Christopher's", there is a large painting of three balloons rising into the sky. It is the work and the gift of three school friends of Christopher, who wanted to create something in his memory before they left prep school. A balloon festival was a regular event at the school and was something which they had all greatly enjoyed together. It is a painting which says such a lot.

For further details about CHASE email info@chasecare.org.uk or visit our website at www.chasecare.org.uk

Head office:
  Loseley Park
  Guildford
  Surrey GU3 1HS
  Tel: 01483 454213
  Fax: 01483 454214

Christopher's
  Old Portsmouth Road
  Guildford
  Surrey GU3 1LP
  Tel: 01483 230960
  Fax: 01483 230961

Registered charity 1042495

# Chapter Two

# About Christopher

Christopher More-Molyneux

## About Christopher

Christopher was 12 years old when he died. He was a much-loved son, brother, grandson and friend to many and 'C' was always wanting to be busy with one of his many interests.

His desire to be busy started on the day he was born. The hospital refused to believe that Sarah was about to deliver. His father was at home walking dogs. Luckily Sarah did know what was happening and after giving the maternity unit a cardiac, on 2nd June 1985, Christopher James More-Molyneux entered this world.

For his first four years he hardly spoke. After all what was the point? He got everything he required through a combination of gesticulations and grunts! Once he had started though, he never stopped.

He had an amazing ability to communicate with young and old alike. Anyone who has been on the receiving end of Christopher's flashing smile seldom seems to forget it.

Jersey cows, Angus his white Westie, his four ferrets – Pete, Strawberry, Pudding and Weasel, were a very important part of Christopher's life. Getting up at 5 am to be with his beloved animals and the farm staff was not a problem as far as Chris was concerned. Going to bed early though sometimes was!

Sport of every kind, from rugger to skiing and shooting to fishing, was all so important and carried out with enthusiasm and interest. Drumming, Art and fly tying all guaranteed to make sure he was never bored.

He was highly competitive, especially in sport, and a dyslexic sufferer, who as a result of good teaching and determination was combating it.

During his last summer holidays he went on a Scripture Union holiday to Monkton Combe. When asked how he got on with the religious element of the week he replied, "Yes, makes you think doesn't it".

Yes, probably more than we realised.

Never a saint but in God's eyes we pray he is safe as an angel.

"When the first baby laughed, for
the first time, the laugh broke into
a thousand pieces, and they all
went skipping about, and that
was the beginning of the fairies"

J M Barrie (1860 - 1937)

# Chapter Three

# Angels, Butterflies, and Things that Fly

## This heaven place

This heaven place sounds good to me
I wonder if you eat cakes and tea
I wonder if you can play with toys
If the playground's filled with girls and boys
I wonder if the flowers grow
If babies really count their toes
If it's filled with ancient kings and queens
Magic fairies with stars and dreams
And if you get fish and chips for tea
Then I guess heaven is the place for me

Don't worry mummy

Don't worry mummy, I'm always here
Even when you have shed a tear
I'll always be there by your heart
So we're never really far apart
Don't worry mummy you've worked real hard
You've always kept me by your guard
Sing a song and we both will sing
I'll still be right there under your wing
Don't worry mummy, I know you care
Cuddle yourself, and we'll both be there
I was in the world, for a short time
But don't worry mummy I will always shine

Drawing by Abbie aged 3

# Find a song

Find a song to remember me
A special song that'll always be
Just play it when you want to find
A special part of me in your mind
Find a song that's good in your ears
That makes the stars shine through your tears
A song where fairies dance in your heart
So we're never really far apart

# The butterfly

My mummy said that when we die
We turn into a butterfly
And when my baby sister died
We all had hugs and cried and cried
So I asked my mummy if we could get
A butterfly to keep as a pet
She said that no this could not be
As butterflies fly high and free
But just the other day I saw
A butterfly outside my door
It was a lovely pretty pink
And it looked at me and gave a wink
She flew about and fluttered round
And landed just upon the ground
She flies by nearly every day
Then flutters off along her way
And when she comes I always kiss her
As I'm sure it is my baby sister

The residents of heaven

I think you'll find in heaven
That it really rather rocks
It comes complete with postmen
Who wear funny coloured socks

There are angel chefs who cook
A lovely Sunday roast
And not to mention the local pub
Who do a lovely cheese on toast

There's a local angel policeman
But his hours are not that long
As the residents of heaven
Never do anything wrong

There are clowns for entertainment
A mouse who likes his cheese
A baboon that laughs and grins all day
And never says thanks or please

A garden full of flowers
A hippopotamus with one eye
A school for angels and magic fairies
To teach them how to fly

An angel who makes daisy chains
And magic golden rings
A silver palace with bells and birds
That's full of queens and kings

There's a place where all the dancing happens
At the local heaven ball
So I think you'll agree, and say with me
That heaven is rather cool

What I will send to you

When you cry for me I'll sing to you
As that is what you used to do
You helped me with my greatest fears
So I'll put fairy dust inside your tears
You loved and cared, you gave up your sleep
So I'll send angels when I see you weep
You protected me and would never moan
So I'll bring you love when you feel alone
You'd give give give, and at no cost
So I'll send silver birds when you're feeling lost
If you've feelings of hurt and disbelief
I'll send you friends to share your grief

# I love you Dad

Dad, now that I have died,
I know it makes you sad
But think of all those loving times
Of love and hugs we've had
I know that our days together
Were far too short and few
But I know that you love me
And that I'll always love you too
Hold onto our memories dad,
They're special ones to keep
I'll be with you throughout your days
And with you when you sleep
Keep our lovely cuddles dad
And my smiles within your heart
I'll hold your hand and walk with you,
So we never are apart
So I love you dad, this isn't fair
And all of this is wrong
But I'll stay close by, to catch your tears
And help you to be strong

When my brother died

When my older brother died
It made me feel all bad inside
But it's OK now I feel just fine
As I know he's with me all the time
And sometimes when I sit in bed
I quietly talk to him in my head
I tell him what I've done at school
And how I think he's really cool
And sometimes when we're feeling brave
We go and visit him at his grave
I'll always say a lovely prayer
Because I know that my brother is still there

Heavenly puddings

The puddings found in heaven
Are the really tasty ones
There's chocolate in banana split
And icing on cream buns

There's cake that's full of vanilla cream
And fluffy icing stuff
The angels and the fairies
Well they just can't get enough

The apple pie is flavoured
With a special kind of sauce
That you only eat, off your feet
Whilst sitting on a horse

The ice creams full of flavours
That you never would expect
The angels make the chocolate cake
With a glitter babe effect

There are profiteroles with custard
And this little goblin man
Who flies around without a sound
Making strawberry jam

The angels in charge of cake making
Have massive mixing spoons
They spend all day and mix away
Whilst helped out by baboons

So the puddings found in heaven
Are really rather yummy
So heaven food, is quite a dude
And sits well inside my tummy!

# Courage

Courage I was introduced to you
By brave and tough and hope
They told me I should stick with you
When it got too hard to cope
Courage you were there, by my side
All the times I felt unwell
When I was ill, you gave me strength
And helped me when I fell
You've picked me up when I was down
You held me by the hand
You showed me how, you got me through
And taught me how to stand
Courage there's a lot to thank you for
You've stood strong beside my side
Thank you for giving me courage
To be strong the day I died
Please take care of my loved ones now
As my friend you'll always be
They need you now, to help them through
The fact that they've lost me
Courage, help them through their pain
Stand upon their fears
Help them to be just like you courage
And sail on through their tears
So courage, you gave me so much courage
You were with me till the end
And with all the things that we've been through
Courage
You are my friend

To my Granny and Granddad

To my Granny and my Granddad
I love you very much
I'll treasure all our memories
Our cuddles and our touch
Our special little moments
Now that I have died
Keep them safe as treasure
In your heart that's deep inside
To my Granny and my Granddad
All the things that you may feel
All the sadness, guilt and anger
All these things I want to heal
So to my Granny and my Granddad
Keep me safe within your heart
I'm your Grandchild and I love you
And that love will never part

# Angels

Angels come in different forms
There are lots of them around
They fly about, some dressed in white
And they hardly make a sound

There are golden glowing loving angels
And ones with flowing wings
There are some with curly wavy hair
And some that love to sing

There are some that love to play the harp
There are some who always glisten
And sometimes you can hear them singing
If you quietly listen

There are guardian angels that stay with you
And when I can't be here
They'll look after you wherever you go
And wipe away your tears

There are some that will just turn right up
When you're in a muddle
Or some that send you waves of love
When you need a cuddle

These angels, well they're everywhere
They can't take away the pain
But they will bring out the shining sun
When your tears turn into rain

So call upon your angels
Go on - give it a try
Just to tell them you need them there
And they might just well reply

"George sitting on a cloud in heaven with an angel, looking down on us"
by Josh aged 6

Babies

Did you know in heaven?
There's a special baby place
They float around and gurgle
With smiles upon their face
They're all so really tiny
And all so very happy
They all have angel wings
And wear an angel nappy
Babies! Babies! Babies!
Whoever invented them?
Such a good idea I think
And in heaven they live again

## Chapter Four

# Stars
# And special things
# Like that

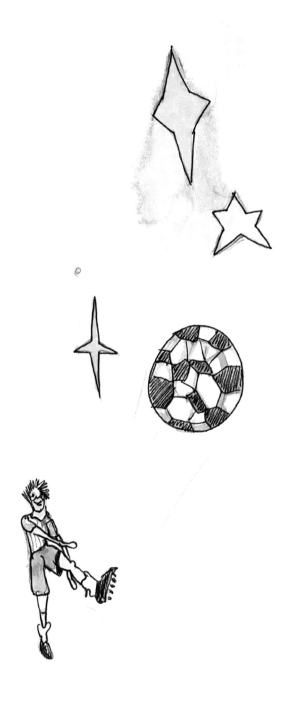

I've just arrived in heaven

I've just arrived in heaven
And it's alright here — you know
It's full of sparkly stars
And pretty things that grow
It's really easy to breathe
As the air is pure and clear
There's candyfloss for children
And for daddies there is beer
There are footballs for the boys
And princesses for the girls
There's a special angel hairdresser
Who looks after plaits and curls
There are fish and chips with peas
And of course tomato sauce
A magic waterfall
And a magic flying horse
But the really bestest bit
About this heaven up above
Is the special kind of feeling
That has filled me up with love

# Look!

Look into a mirror
Just look at what you see
Fairies in your eyes
Well that bit, that is me!

Look harder at your eyes
Now look through all those tears
There's dancing little pixies
And my voice inside your ears

Now look now deep within
Our souls are in our heart
They are beating now as one
So we'll never be apart

# Dad

Dear Dad you've been my hero
You've helped me through my years
You've cared for me just like Dads do
So I'll help you with your tears

You've been there when I needed you
You've helped me through and through
You've shown me love and brought me strength
Just like the best dads do

We've laughed together, we've shared our jokes
Dad, you're my best friend
So you and me, we'll always have
Something special that'll never end

So Dad you've been my hero
Keep me safe within your heart
As where you go, I'll stay close by
Two heroes, never apart

"Angel of Bliss" for George by Jack aged 13

# To My brother

To my very special brother
I know that I have died
I know it makes you sad
And I know that you have cried

I know that you feel mad
And that none of this is fair
But I want you now to know
That I'm always always there

Remember all our good times
All our smiles and our fun
All the times we laughed and played
All the cheeky things we've done!

Play some of my music
To help you think of me
I'll sing along — you just won't hear
Your side I'll always be

So talk to me when you need me
And I'll do my best to send
A hug to my bestest brother
Who's also my best friend

You know what people say?

You know that people say
That often when you die
You turn into a bird
Or a pretty butterfly
You know that people say
You might sit upon a star
That you float upon a cloud
Or you twinkle up and far
That you turn into an angel
That the moon you fly around
That you scatter fairy dust
And dance upon the ground
You know that people say
When you die you shine right through
Well now that I have died
I can tell you its all true

What happens when you die?

What happens when you die?
How do we try and believe
When your heart stops its beating
When you no longer have to breathe
Life could be like a circle
That starts off when we're born
And that however big the circles made
Another can be drawn
Maybe it's like a ship
As she travels for all to see
But is heading for the horizon
Between the sky and sea
We watch so very closely
As she moves along her way
As gradually we lose sight of her
And she slowly slips away
So she may be gone from our sight
But the thing that we do know
Is that there's someone waiting the other side
To greet her as she goes
So maybe we should try to remember
Although it feels so hard and numb
That when we lose a life in nature
Somewhere else it has just begun

# The pearly gates!

You know the story about the pearly gates?
Well I tell you it's all true
I arrived there just the other day
And well I didn't have a clue
But an angel came to greet me
And said "Hang on here, please wait"
She gave me my very own halo
And then let me through the gate
She looked down at my shoes
And said "You can't come in in those
In heaven" she said "We have bare feet
And you might tread on someone's toes"
She handed me my heaven box
And on the front was written 'STARS'
And when I opened it up, inside
I found several magic jars
"In one" she said "Are fairies
They'll put love upon your face
And in another there are stars
To create magic in this place
In this one" she said "Are lollipops
And sweets and sweets galore
And when you've eaten them all up" she said
"It will just fill up with some more
And then" she said, "In this one
Now this one's full of love
You're to use this jar of treasure
To send love from here above"
So if you need a cuddle from me
You just look up in the sky
As my little jar of love here
It has an endless supply!

# Now I've died

I died the other day
But it really wasn't bad
My mum and dad they cried
As I think it made them sad

Just before I died
We spent some time together
They said that they would always
Love me now forever

At first I was quite scared
As I didn't want to die
It made me very sad
And it made me want to cry

But now that it has happened
My fear has gone away
Mum and dad can't see me
But I'm with them everyday

I want them both to know
That I'll hug all of their fears
That it's still ok to cry
As I'll mop up all their tears

Quiet thoughts of me

What's your favourite thought?
Of me that's in your head
That makes you smile and grin
Or cry tears for me instead
Is there something little?
A poem or a rhyme
A walk amongst nature
To remind you of our time
A song that's on the radio
A favourite CD
A photo or a drawing
To help you think of me
Whatever it may be
Cherish it like treasure
And our special little moments
Will be with you forever

"For Anthony to get where he's going safely" by Darren aged 16

## Dreams

Have you ever dreamed a dream?
That really made you feel
As if you were right there alive
And that you wanted to be real
Have you ever seen a star?
That twinkles out so bright
That creates a special sparkle
And magic kind of light
As on clear star studded nights
If you look up at the skies
You'll find a magic twinkle
Reflecting in your eyes
Then as you fall asleep
The thing that I will do
Is catch the really bright ones
And make your dreams come true

## Dear Daddy

Dear daddy please don't worry
I haven't gone that far
When you cry for me I'll sing
And touch you from my star
I'll be there when you grieve
And when you're feeling sad
I'll bring you lots of love
When you're alone and feeling bad
You're a very special daddy
As I know you always cared
So dear daddy please don't worry
As your love was never spared

A heaven full of animals!

In heaven there are animals
A fantastic looking crowd
The only trouble is, is that
They're really rather loud

The monkeys they wear bobble hats
And big red fluffy slippers
While the little baby elephants
Are naughty little nippers

The giraffes, they play the violin
The parrots play the drums
The mice all smell and play the bells
Whilst eating chocolate buns

The pigs, they wear funny hats
Ride horses and do lancing
The hamsters laugh and look quite daft
And like to go line dancing

The butterflies are very special
They're full of lovely love
They sing away throughout the day
Whilst wearing pretty gloves

The dogs and cats eat beans on toast
And are friends with all the bees
They make their money by making honey
Whilst goats all make the cheese

So the animals in heaven
I think that you'll agree
Make it all a heavenly ball
And a lovely place to be

# Mummy

Mummy I know you miss me
As we had that special bond
If things just had been different
If we could wave a magic wand
But we both know that we can't
And that this is what life's about
It's just hard to understand
And it makes you scream and shout
Mummy I know you miss me
Well I'm here with you right now
That's also hard to understand
As I know you're asking how?
Talk to me now mummy
Tell me all your fears
Tell me how you miss me
And I'll help you with your tears
Take me with you places
That we would have never seen
Talk to me — you still can
And I'll treasure where we've been
So I know you miss me mummy
But all that I can say
Is that I am still by your side
And will be with you all the way

# Beautiful!

Beautiful is the word
That's used for little ones
For little princess daughters
And lovely little sons
Beautiful little babies
With tiny hands and feet
Beauty is that every one
Is really quite unique
Beautiful when on earth
And then even when they die
Beautiful! Beautiful! And more beautiful!
In heaven in the sky

# Chapter Five

# Flowers...
# ...that talk

# Letters to Heaven

The postmen here in heaven
Why they never ever fail
To get to you in first class time
All the heaven mail

It arrives in heaps and sacks
From the people that we love
Special words in letters
That are sent right here above

The postmen whiz about all day
Delivering all the post
And have heaven competitions
As to who can do the most

People send us letters here
To tell us what they wish
To tell us how they're feeling
And to tell us that we're missed

So write some special words to me
Even though we are apart
And I'll send mine, right in disguise
As love, straight to your heart

I'm with you every day

Remember all the kisses
And hugs that we have had
The times you gave me cuddles
When I was feeling sad
Well all those lovely ways
They don't all have to end
Because although you cannot see me
These things I will still send
A cuddle with a pet
A hug with a best friend
A twinkle from a star
That shows there is no end
A lovely special dream
A rainbow in the sky
A brightness from a flower
That helps me catch your eye
The way that something happens
A nice smell that's in the home
And a magical slight breeze
Is a kiss that I have blown

# My Sister

My sister, she's the best thing to me
We laugh, we sing, we dance with glee
We're close you see, we share so much
I love her laugh I love her touch
The way she smiles, the way she shops
The way her giving never stops
Her lovely hair her pretty face
It brightens up every darkened space
My sister, she has cancer you see
But she'll always be so special to me
Her courage, strength, her soul inside
It's something precious she'll never hide
In fact she's passed her soul onto me
My beautiful sister is what she'll always be
But I'll never forget the day I cried
On the day that my special sister died

The little things that keep you going

It might only be little
But it's the little things that count
Something someone says
It needn't be a large amount
A comment from a friend
A hug that squeezes tight
An ear just to listen
In the middle of the night
A favourite song to play
A favourite song to hear
A caring few words
A bowl to catch a tear
A touching friendly card
That sends to you a thought
A beautiful bunch of flowers
A smile that someone brought
A poem that you've read
A cooked meal for you to eat
It's the little things that count
To keep you on your feet
So the little things that happen
The things that people do
Are the things to hold in your darkest times
The things to get you through

# Flowers in my heaven

There are flowers in my heaven
But they're special ones you know
They change colour and make magic
And sparkle when they grow

There are flowers in my heaven
And they do smell very sweet
I think if heaven had no flowers
It wouldn't be complete

There are flowers in my heaven
And the other day I thought
That I heard one give a whisper
And then I heard it talk

So there are flowers in my heaven
They'd smell delicious in a bunch
But I might just pick the best ones
And then eat them for my lunch

# Flowers

There's this lovely place in heaven
That's FILLED with lovely flowers
I wonder how long they took to plant
I expect it was hours and hours

Drawing by Emma aged 14

## Coping

Coping is just something you do
It's never really planned
People who don't have to cope
Why they just don't understand
They say things like
"Oh I don't know how you cope"
"I don't know how you do it"
"I couldn't, I'd have lost my hope"
But it doesn't really work like that
You find ways of coping where
You didn't think it possible
And ways you never thought were there
So coping
Well you just do it
And that's that
It's not clever; it's not a well done

It's just something you do

# Pain

Pain you're such a painful thing
That's hurts you deep inside
A throbbing pain inside your soul
That's there when someone dies

Pain, why do you beat my heart?
Why do you drain my soul?
Why do you punch and kick at me?
Pain, you take your toll

You're a pain that's indescribable
Pain, why are you here?
Pain, you're one big battle
That makes me feel my fears

The loss that I have suffered
It really does not compare
As pain, in my hardest hours
I know that you'll be there

You tire me out, you are a strain
You are a giant struggle
You are a battleground of hurt
You are a jigsaw muddled

So pain, please tell me what to do
Tell me, as I can't see
How do I drain you away pain?
What have you done with me?

# Talking flowers

Have you ever seen a flower?
That really caught your eye
That made you feel all cheery
And say how bright! Oh my!
Did you ever see a flower?
While out on a leisurely walk
Did you ever try and whisper
To see if it might talk
Well next time you see a flower
(One that's really bright)
That makes the face of heaven
Have flowers all in sight
Make sure you are alone
Then talk to it and see
As it may just then talk back to you
If it's bright and sent by me!

# My best friend

My best friend died, her heart it stopped
Her life came to an end
Her soul it lifted from her shell
She died
I've lost my friend

Friends forever we always said
We'd talk for hours on end
We'd both get married, be super stars
She died
I've lost my friend

We'd play we'd laugh we'd dance and sing
Each others broken hearts we'd mend
Our smiles, our giggles, our holding hands
She died
I've lost my friend

We'd do our hair and makeup
And we never could pretend
We shared our secrets that no one else knew
She died
I've lost my friend

So my best friend died, my heart will cry
So many things I want to send
My love, my world, my life, my dreams
You died
I've lost my friend

# Cuddles

Cuddles are a giant hug
Of love that you can bring
Oh a cuddle is so lovely
And just such a cuddly thing
A cuddle is just something you give
When someone needs a cry
A cuddly way to say you care
Or just to get them by
A cuddle comforts pain and sadness
And when your mind's in trouble
I suggest a huge ginormous
Loving lovely cuddle
Having a really good cuddle
Is nicer than chocolate cake
In fact it's nicer than apple pie
And you never put on weight
So cuddles are a marvellous invention
They're hugs with an added snuggle
So go on, find a cuddly friend
To give you one cuddly cuddle

Babies are just like flowers

Babies are just like flowers
Beautiful little blooms
They put a smile upon my face
And brighten up our rooms

I really do love babies
And then I love flowers too
But if they were exactly alike
Then whatever would we do?

As I really can't imagine
If flowers wee'd and poo'd
I mean if a flower burped in my house
I'd think it terribly rude

Then they both do smell delicious
And yummy scrummy to me
So I could just save them both
And eat them for my tea

But if my baby can't be here
A flower is what they'd be
A really beautiful lovely one
That's bright for all to see

So babies are just like flowers
They're small but big and bright
and I know my special little baby
will put flowers all in sight

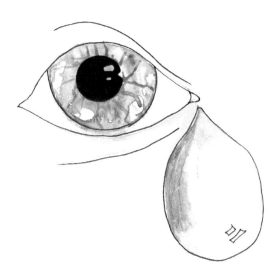

## Tears

Tears are very special things
That glisten when you cry
They trickle down your cheek
After falling from your eye
But then I've often wondered
If your eyes never had tears
Where would all that sadness go?
Would it come out of your ears?
As whoever invented people
Must have thought quietly in their brain
That for all the sadness that people bear
Well it needs somewhere to drain
So tears are what they made
They pour down from your eye
A release of pain and sadness
A release to make you cry
And although crying is tiring
It lets out hurt and fears
So make use of the invention
Of those special things called tears

## Dear you, from me

Why have I lost my precious one? My eyes have cried and cried
It makes no sense, so hard to bear, why is it that you died?
Why is it that you left me, why have you gone away?
I miss you so so much, and more than words can say
I just can't carry on like this, I'm so alone without you here
And every time I think of you, my heart then cries a tear
This world just isn't fair and I just don't understand
What I'd give to touch you and just hold your precious hand

I hear you mum, don't worry, I know this isn't fair
I know you really miss me, and I know that you do care
But I've had to leave this world a bit sooner than we planned
I want to help you grieve and to help you understand
Although you cannot see me and touch me everyday
I'm with you all the time and I'll be with you all the way
I'm always going to be there, I'll hold you when you weep
I'll cuddle right up next to you when I see you sleep
I'll walk with you through life, I'll join you when you sing
I'll send you love and comfort, and the good times I will bring
So don't think of me as gone, I'm always always here
And in so many subtle ways, my love it will appear
So keep going mum through life, together we will be
Our love, our souls, our hearts, our dreams
Joined as one
You
And me

# Alone

Mummy I know you feel alone
And the loss is too hard to explain
I know the hurt is unbearable
And your heart is numb with pain

Mummy I know you feel alone
I see you struggle every day
I see you cry and lie awake at night
When friends don't know what to say

Mummy I know you feel alone
I can feel all of your fears
But cuddles and hugs they're good things mummy
And they help bring out your tears

Mummy I know you feel alone
But you're not alone you see
I'll send loving friends to share your grief
And I'll send you love from me

# The Pop Star Place

There's this pop star place in heaven
That's full of music stars
They dance and sing in glitter frocks
And drive round in posh cars

They make music that is rocking
And sing out boogie grooves
They practise hard their dance routines
And show their pop star moves

There are angel stars that sing
Eat chocolate pop star buns
There's one that plays the trumpet
And one that rocks the drums

There's a bit where all the famous ones
Hang out and eat posh food
There's an angel pop star palace
That is just for coolest dudes

The Famous pop star angels
Why they really are the best
As all the really coolest ones
Will sing right on request

You get given your own stereo
And your very best CD
A microphone for Karaoke
And pop star cups of tea

So this pop star place in heaven
Although when you die it's sad
You can sing and dance whenever you like
And oogie boogie mad

"Laura" by Laura aged 17

# It's OK

It's ok to hurt and ok to cry
To say your prayers and say goodbye
It's ok to laugh yet feel despair
To take your grief and talk and share
It's ok to feel such awful pain
That is just too hard to try and explain
It's ok to lose your only hope
To say it's hard and too much to cope
It's ok to feel in such a muddle
To hold a hand and have a cuddle

Sock Shop by Patti, Janette, Paul, Donna, Angela, Elaine and Dan

Chapter Six

# Chocolate
# Socks
# For
# Caterpillars

my sock

Wodder codder language

Wodder codder bodder boo
Skitter titter tatt
When you die you have to speak
Funny just like that

Skittle brittle ickle tickle
Riddle diddle dee
I'm not sure really what it means
But it sounds ok to me



Fish and chips

When I eat fish and chips
I think of my sister
That's what she used to like eating
I really miss her

She died you see
And I always will miss her
But it's ok, because when I eat fish and chips
I think of my sister

# Caterpillars

Caterpillars like to eat
And gobble up and munch
Leaves and greenish things like that
For breakfast tea and lunch

When caterpillars aren't caterpillars
Like us, they sort of die
They go from being a caterpillar
To a shining butterfly

I wonder if that when they died
They'd still be quite as keen
To munch and gobble and enjoy
Eating up their greens


# The Funny Ant

When I went to heaven
I met this funny ant
Who only ate bananas
And liked to rave and rant

So one day I asked him
Why he liked to rave and rant
He replied, "Why it is of course
That I'm a funny ant"

"My Butterfly" by Ben aged 4

# The smelly giraffe

When I died I met this friendly
Tall and smelly giraffe
So I told him even though he'd died
He still should take a bath

# Heaven Language

Have you ever thought?
About the way you have to talk
Like should you speak in heaven?
With an accent like in Devon
Like a policeman from a land
That's full of snow and sand
Like a bird from silly sally
Or a snail from dilly dally
Like a tiger who's in trouble
Or a cat that hubble bubbles
A mermaid in Peru
Or a man that lost his shoe
Like a dentist with a brace
Or a frog from outer space
A rabbit that's in bed
With a headache in his head
Like a postman with a medal
And a bike with just one pedal
So now that we have thought
About the way we have to talk
Like when you get to heaven
And you count up to eleven
I think that when I die
And there are angels in the sky
I'll dibble dabble slight
And just talk the way I like

Sweet money

You can't spend money in heaven
You're not allowed
The manager of the bank
Is quite frank
About the fact you can only buy
Things in heaven with sweets


Favourite food

When you die
You go to this place
Where you get all your favourite food
And stuff your face
And when you've stuffed your face
You stuff your tummy
With all the things you find yummy
And then your legs and your arms
And if you can, your ears too
So even though when you die it's sad
It's ok because you get to eat
All your favourite food
Whenever you like

Smelly or jelly?

Heaven is filled with all the things
That you find you love the most
Mine is filled with dogs and cats
And chocolate sauce on toast

My friend said hers is filled with cheese
Which I find rather smelly
So I suggested that she changed her mind
And filled it up with jelly

"My idea of heaven" by Jade aged 12

# The laughing place

There's this place called the laughing place
That's way up in the sky
Where no one can stop laughing
However hard they try
They giggle higgle happy
They tickle tee hee ho
They hoo hoo ha ha diddle
And tee hee toe tum toe
So way up in this laughing place
I think that you will see
They're giggle happy wacky
And ho ho tee hee hee

Drawing by Sam

Jiggle wiggle diggle dum

Jiggle wiggle diggle dum
Chiggle iggle chews
I know for a fact that when you die
You get chocolate socks and shoes



Nonsense land

Do you think that when you die?
You go to a land that bakes lots of pie
Where custard tarts and milkshake drinks
Play snakes and ladders and tiddly winks
Where forks and cups and plates and spoons
Bake cakes and cookies with baboons
Do you think that when you die?
You go to a place where elephants fly
Where cows go "baa" and sheep say "moo"
Where the sky is green and the grass is blue
Do you think that when you die?
You diddle um pum and riddle dee lie
Well wherever you go and whatever you'll be
I expect you'll get something, nice for your tea

"My idea of heaven" by Luke aged 10

## The friendly place

When you go to heaven
There are friendly people around
Who make sure you're looked after
And that when you're lost you're found

When you go to heaven
There is a friendly bear
Who's really good at plaiting
And puts pony tails in hair

When you go to heaven
There is a friendly bee
Who makes you whatever you want
To have that day for tea

And when you go to heaven
There is this laundry fox
Who washes all your t-shirts
And all your smelly socks


## Telly

I wonder if that when you die
You still can watch the telly
I'd rather eat some ice cream though
And raspberry flavoured jelly

"The helloello person" by heather aged 5

## Helloelloyou land

When you die there's a little place
Called helloelloyou
It's full of helloello people
Who say helloello to you
They're friendly helloello people
Who yellow mellow too
So when you die you yellow mellow
helloelloyou


## Chocolate

Chocolate heaven is really great
There's chocolate spoons and chocolate plates
There's even chocolate cabbages
And chocolate televisions
And all the things on the television are chocolate too
As in heaven
Everything is chocolate
Everything except jars of strawbriladelephant jam
Because that would just be silly

"Take him and cut him out in little stars and he will make the face of heaven so fine that all the world will be in love with night"

Shakespeare

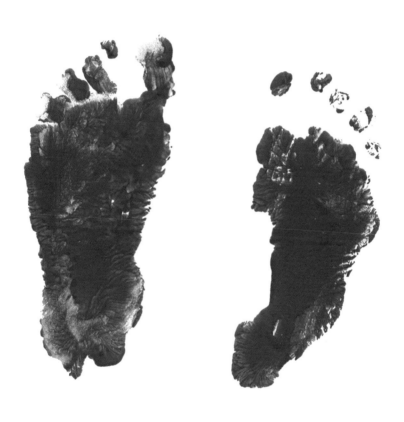

"My Feet" by Ben aged 8 months

## Chapter Seven

# Julia's Story

HELLO

Drawings by Julia

# Julia's story

This is a story about courage, determination, cheerfulness and hope in a young girl whose concern for others often outweighed her concern for herself. She was brave yet scared, she was intelligent and wanting to know what was happening to her body, what the consequences of taking the drugs were and whether there were any alternatives that would have less side effects. She wanted to know the whys and ifs in order to weigh up whether it was what she wanted, but most of all she wanted to live and overcome her disease. The disease being a rare form of cancer known as Ewing's Sarcoma.

She asked, "Why me, I don't cause any problems?" her answer was, "I know, God knows I believe in him and he is using me to show others how to be brave, he knows I can cope with this."

She did cope, she fought hard and long to survive her illness rarely complaining to others, always putting on a brave face. There is hardly a picture without her infectious smile. She fought to have a normal life, but what upset her was her hair loss. What would her classmates think of her, how could she go to school without hair, would they laugh at her? They were in fact most protective and caring towards her. Having lost her hair she wore different hats until someone gave her a blue cap that became her trademark. She tried a wig but found it too hot for most daywear even removing it during a lesson by ducking under the desk when the tutor's back was turned. The tutor's face was evidently a picture.

One bonfire night with a wig in place topped by a hat, watching fireworks she leant too far back and the wig slipped off to the stunned silence of a group of boys behind. They looked as if they had just seen an alien! Julia thought this was very funny.

Normal to Julia meant attending school at every possible moment. She would come out of chemotherapy on a Sunday and be in school on the Monday, happy to be with her friends and tutors. Fiercely independent she would try to manage her haversack complete with what seemed like the kitchen sink from classroom to classroom. Her friends took pleasure in being bag carriers; often the bag would arrive before she did. In between chemo's she often had infections and had to stay in her local hospital. Here she became well known for her sense of humour and cartoon drawing of the staff, their expressions dependant upon whether they were going to allow her to go home or not. She built up a good rapport with her consultant who had been known to enter the room waving a white handkerchief because he knew that her blood counts were not good enough to allow her to go home. These were friendly and warm exchanges. Sometimes compromises were made.

Julia had to have various operations to put in place a Hickman line for the admission of drugs, and a gastrostomy tube for feeding, as her weight had dropped so dramatically, several bone marrow retrievals and an operation for a spacer. The spacer allowed her to have a high dose radiation to her pelvis without causing damage to  her internal organs. This operation took place in a North London hospital and she had to be in for a week so visiting had been difficult for her friends. On returning to school her class had seen her arrive from their form room window. Suddenly 24 girls burst through the outside door to greet Julia. She was swallowed up by them and taken into class, one girl going to report that she was in whilst others took her bag. I was left to find my way back to the car alone!

Her friends in school were amazing. They saw Julia as Julia, not as someone who was ill and needing special treatment. They cared and provided her with love and support, did not see the loss of hair or the tubes as making her any different. When she was in hospital having chemo they came to visit or sent cards, emails, and texts or telephoned. They always informed her of the latest gossip. This she appreciated, as when she returned to school she would fit in with them knowing what had been happening.

Julia's final chemo treatment was due after Christmas 2001. I had unfortunately been admitted to hospital just before Christmas with gastroenteritis. Julia took on the role of getting the house ready for Christmas finding the decorations and putting up the tree for my return on Christmas Eve. Her treatment day came and as I was still unwell she stoically suggested that she should stay in hospital by herself as long as I would go up at bedtime. Friends visited during the day and I was taken to see her at bedtime only to be told five minutes after arriving, "It's alright now you can go as I want to see Eastenders, then I'm going to chat to the others." So I went home.

The high dose chemo was set for January 2002. In fact she was in hospital for her 12th birthday. Friends, neighbours, family, nurses and tutors were very kind, sending cards and presents. The night nurses made a happy birthday sign for her door, which thrilled her. I had had the night off; to create the cake and daddy had stayed. The cake was topped with two creatures, one named Boo, the other Dermot who represented two of the doctors caring for Julia and shared her quirky sense of humour. I arrived with cake, food and drink for her party. Well we partied all day. Her whole class phoned during their break to sing happy birthday and speak to her. We had a string of friends after school all of whom tried the highlight of the birthday presents – a pair of trainers with wheels that could be retracted. Julia had used the long corridor as a speedway, the best bit was that she was attached to a drip stand, which she used to steady herself. The nurses were almost having heart attacks but she smiled cheekily at them as she continued on her way. Luckily there were no mishaps for her, her friends however found it more difficult despite support from Julia and the drip stand they still managed to topple over.

After the wonderful birthday we continued with the high dose with its unpleasant side effects. During one particularly long day and night when she was very poorly being sick for what seemed like the hundredth time that day, she said, "Well at least I've got something in my tummy to come out because I'm being fed through my tube". She had had a feeding tube inserted (gastrostomy) some months earlier as her weight was so low and she needed to be nourished.

During Julia's stay in hospital for the operation to put in the spacer she had to have an epidural to help with the pain, during the first few hours when everyone thought she would be groggy Julia needed the loo. "I'll be alright to walk to the toilet", she said as the nurse arrived with a wheelchair. She soon found out that it wasn't possible to stand, let alone walk, and gracefully accepted a ride in the chair.

By the Thursday she was raring to be up, so the physiotherapist came with crutches in the morning, saying that if she coped well with them they would help her tackle the stairs in the afternoon. Well there was a challenge, she was determined to be stair walking that afternoon and out of hospital by the Friday. It was important for her to be discharged because we had tickets to see one of her friends in the school play, The Red Balloon, and yes we did make it complete with crutches.

During her five and a half weeks of intensive radiotherapy she had to attend hospital daily. This routine was planned around her school life. On one occasion; she had to attend a clinic in the morning and asked if she could be out by lunchtime, because she was walking round her school field for charity. We were back in time for this event. I only realized later that she had undertaken this walk every day for a week. Her year tutor did phone to ask if it was alright for her to do this, feeling 'well jolly good for you Julia for showing a good example of helping others, despite not being well yourself', but at the same time concerned for her well being.

By July 2002 we thought we had conquered the disease, her bone marrow results were looking good and she had put on weight. Her Hickman line and spacer had been removed although we were waiting a date for the removal of the feeding tube.

I can remember her joy when she learnt that things were looking good. She texted her friends, insisted that we called on her grandparents and godmother with the news, even texted her nurses at the local hospital.

We went on holiday to Cumbria using her godfather's cottage. We had super weather and Julia was full of energy and fun. She rowed on Windermere, and tried rock climbing. She loved it and planned to find a club local to home when she returned so that she could continue this sport. She was looking forward to returning to school in September with her newly grown hair but she had developed a lump on her head. After several visits to the hospital we were told that the disease had returned. We were devastated.

After much discussion it was decided that she would have radiotherapy on the lump and it disappeared but bone marrow results were not good. So we were offered a chance to go on a trial programme of a new type of chemotherapy in the hope that this would have a more lasting effect. Julia was keen especially if the results could help other people with the disease. She had always had an ambition to be a research doctor in the hope that she could find a cure for some disease or other. In September Julia did manage the first three weeks of school but suddenly found it difficult to cope and then stayed at home. She began to lose confidence. It was at this time when things had reached a low that a good friend introduced us to Christopher's Children's Hospice.

Elaine from the hospice came to visit; I had come home from hospital to meet her whilst Julia's godmother entertained her. Elaine explained in her very reassuring way how the hospice worked. The set up sounded ideal but we were apprehensive at the word hospice, so we visited. From the moment we walked through the doors we were enveloped in an atmosphere of fun, comfort and love. Everything was bright; the facilities were fantastic from the pool to the sensory room to the beautifully furnished rooms. It was arranged for Julia to go down for a visit. Before our visit we met Tania, who arrived in a silver beetle car sporting white painted flowers. Well, Julia was impressed. Not only that, Tania only looked like a sixth former. Julia's first visit was great. She enjoyed the facilities, the sensory room becoming her favourite place. Whilst there her nasal tube had to be replaced; not something she liked having done but she gave the nurses 10 plus.

The months went on. Julia was encouraged to return to school by friends and tutors some of whom phoned to explain the exciting things that were going on including a Latin party. Well, the thought of a party in Latin was a decider. We have some wonderful photographs of girls wearing sheets and being fed grapes. Julia's attendance at school became irregular, she worked at home with a tutor. Remarkably she managed to keep up with her work even doing well in tests.

One day we had a request that two of her tutors wished to see her. They brought the news that she was to receive an award at Prize Giving for bravery and courage. Well we were surprised and delighted that our daughter had been given this award. Julia whilst delighted was her usual unassuming self-commenting, "I have not been particularly brave have I?" Just before the day of the prize giving Julia was unwell and we were a little unsure whether she would make it but she was well enough to attend. When her name was announced and she stood up to receive the prize the warmth and applause was quite overwhelming to us.

By December we had discovered that the new treatment was not keeping the cancer at bay. So we tried another treatment, which entailed me giving injections at home. By now she was finding it difficult to walk and she had reverted to using crutches. One day Tania suggested a shopping expedition by wheel chair. Julia emphatically said no. Tania was able to persuade her that it could be used as a trolley for the shopping. From then on we were able to use the chair for school visits and outings. The first chair we had was so heavy and cumbersome. PONT (paediatric outreach nursing team) from our local hospital suggested a lightweight chair, which Julia would be able to wheel herself. She was delighted at this as she would be mobile. The chair was quickly personalized with stickers of dogs.

As Julia's disease spread she found life more difficult. She still found the energy to go out on good days. She even took up her duties as an acolyte at church. The girls wanted to give her a Christmas treat so they came up with the idea of a party at her home. Whilst Julia was at a hospital appointment mums came and busied themselves preparing the house for the party. I put up the tree and the table was made festive. On her arrival at home Julia wanted to know why there were mothers in our kitchen and dining room. We managed to sidetrack her by getting her to finish off decorating the tree. The doorbell rang and the girls in Christmas costumes, carrying lanterns began singing carols. Julia was delighted. They had all bought a decoration for her to put on a swag for the stairs. Julia did not want to do this on her own which was the plan. After much persuasion her friends joined in to decorate the swag. We have a joyful video of the girls creating their swag and hanging it on the stairs. Even more hilarity came after supper whilst the adults cleared up. They played murder in the dark; the shrills, squeaks of laughter were music to our ears.

Christmas was only a few days away when infection struck again putting us back in hospital. Right up until Christmas Eve we were not sure if Julia was coming home or whether we would have Christmas in hospital. Julia used her usual charm and threats on her consultant. Although still on antibiotics she was allowed home as PONT kindly agreed to administer the drugs at home during Christmas. Over Christmas she was well, having fun opening her presents and generally littering the house with paper and contents. She took great joy in giving everyone gifts that she had bought and wrapped. After Christmas we were again in hospital with the infection. Luckily we were out by New Year's Eve when we had our usual visit to her Godmother's. She was full of fun, laughter and gaiety. Even playing charades at 2.30 AM when the adults were wanting to go to bed but the children were still full of life.

In January Julia had to undergo more radiotherapy, this time to her face, which involved having to wear a tight fitting mask. She found this uncomfortable but she made a joke about it and took "Lord of the Rings" to listen to while treatment was carried out. To us it was obvious that she was in pain. She disliked having her pain relief increased but after careful negotiation we increased the dose.

Her thirteenth birthday arrived. Determined to enjoy the day she went to school in order to give out cakes only to find that they had organised a party for her. Members of staff joined the girls who were given an extension of their break. On her return home she burst through the door with Tania in tow full of excitement and bubble. Later that day we had our usual family tea with neighbours and friends and cake. This year's cake had thirteen dogs. Dogs were Julia's passion. She wanted one, but in spite of endless trips to dog homes all the dogs she liked were already reserved. The dog had to be a rescue dog as she said they needed good homes having had a bad time and ending up in a dog's home.

Another of Julia's passions was raising money for good causes. She and her form at junior school raised money by having a desktop sale for conservation of the rainforest in South America. She had a drive sale for the RSPCA. In 2001 she and a friend organised and ran a tombola for the Marsden hospital and again in 2002 she had a coffee morning for the Marsden. For this she and her friends made many of the gifts and cards that were sold. This trait seems to have been passed onto her form. They have recently raised £5750 in her memory for Christopher's Hospice by organising a dog walk with each dog having its own sponsor form, and selling some 2300 ice creams in school. This is a heart-warming tribute to our daughter.

The knowledge of Julia's love for dogs spread far and wide and although she never owned one she managed throughout her illness to be surrounded by dogs. From Monty, Sassy, Percy to Dotty and her six pups who were born in November 2002. She went doggie walking with Feenie, the pups came to visit. Even in her last few days of life Dilys a pup came to visit her in hospital. Dilys also had a special invitation from our rector to the celebration of Julia's life in our church.

By the beginning of March Julia's breathing had become more difficult and she now needed oxygen. This we thought might curb her outings because she needed to have an oxygen tube in her nose but this was not so. Her opinion was if you've got it, flaunt it, and that meant the oxygen tube as well.

The weekend of March 8th brought a sleepover for Julia and four friends at Christopher's having first been to the hospital for radiation then to school to finish a pot that she was making. Julia had started her pot a few lessons after the others and she thought that she might not be allowed to make a full sized one but her determination and hard work meant that within two weeks she not only made up for lost time but had also overtaken some of the others. She had to take her oxygen with her but the oxygen cylinder had to be left outside

"Dilys" by Julia's friend Patsy

the art room because of the equipment in the room. Julia set to with great diligence and effort to complete the pot. We left school, pot ready for firing, to drive to Christopher's. Her friends were due the following day.

The weekend was fabulous. The girls were delighted with the hospice, joining in with the activities and helping others who were there. They went ice-skating complete with wheelchair and a nosebleed. They had a thrilling surprise when Tamsin Outhwaite visited, joining them in their favourite sensory room. This surprise had been arranged by the Hospice. This turned out to be the last weekend when she was well enough to enjoy herself. One would never believe how ill she was at the time as the photographs reflect someone who is really enjoying herself.

Julia was now unable to manage the stairs so we made a bedroom for her downstairs; she was not too keen on this as she felt that this was causing too much trouble for everyone. This room became the focal point of home life. The room was often filled with a stream of visitors who talked, read or just sat with her. One day our new rector, Shirley arrived and we had an impromptu service using the commode chair as an altar. This scandalised Julia but she also found it amusing telling her friends that they were sitting on the altar.

On Sunday 16th March Julia was admitted to hospital with a chest infection. After a difficult night she rallied and seemed brighter, antibiotics were administered in the hope that she would overcome the infection. She was her usual undemanding self and very grateful to the nurses who had to help her with every process of daily life. Yet despite finding it difficult to speak she still had a joke for everyone and still drew her cartoons.

After a brave and gallant fight she slipped away very quietly on 19th March. Aged 13.

We were extremely fortunate in that Christopher's have a wonderful Mistral room. This is a room where children can be placed until their funeral.

We were privileged to be allowed to use it. She was taken from our local hospital straight to this room, where she had been placed by the time we arrived, numb with grief. We found her in an ordinary bed surrounded by her soft toys and with her tape playing; to us it was just as if she was sleeping. This special time at Christopher's gave family, our friends and us time to say goodbye slowly and with great dignity. We were very much supported by the staff during our stay. They were there to talk to; they helped us cope with the arrangements for the funeral and even helped us to create the service sheet.

We received hundreds of tributes, some from people who we did not know but all commented about the effect Julia had had on their lives. Julia would have been very humbled to know this. Her friends at school gave an assembly as their tribute to her. Many wrote very moving poems and pieces, which they read in a beautiful service at school. They also contributed to her funeral service by reading pieces and in the celebration of Julia's life, by writing prayers, reading their written piece, and performing a musical tribute.

Although Julia is no longer with us her presence is still felt by those who knew and loved her. She left behind a shining example of how to overcome adversity without complaint, how to take on what life has to offer and use it well. She was, as her Head said to the school, the epitome of the phrase living every moment to the full. More recently in a letter from her school it was said that Julia is still very much with us in so many ways, something that gives us much pleasure and we are sure it would gladden her heart to know that she still works for the good of the school. As a school friend said "How I miss her determination, her merry laugh, her kindness, and I will miss it until I hear it again up in the place she belongs." Another school friend said "She had a strong sense of what was right and what was wrong, however she did like Lucius Malfoy from Harry Potter, which is quite ironic because he is such a villain". Another friend said "You can keep an eye on me from above making sure I am not doing anything stupid." A classmate wrote

You planted your love in so many people
Just as the daffodils scatter their seeds in so many places

Your imprint is everywhere
The rainforest
The moon
And in our hearts
But you still kept smiling
Cheerful
To the very end
Your pain is over now
But ours is just beginning.

She was a peacemaker, caring very much about others both human and animal.

Perhaps her own poem written in 2000 sums her up.

A New Millennium should be a new start
A time to reflect on the wrong things we have done
A time to stop wars and poverty
A time to stop sadness
An end to child abuse
Everyone should be friends
Kind to each other
Everyone should resolve to try harder
So this world can be a better place
For everyone to work and play in
Everyone should be safe wherever they are.

So ends the story of our beloved precious daughter, our only child, a story that hopefully portrays Julia's determination to be cheerful and understanding of others' needs, and show courage and sensitivity throughout her battle with cancer.

GOODBYE

# Thank you!

Many people have helped make this book what it is now. The heart of this book comes from the people who matter the most, these inspirational families, as without them and their shared experiences this book would have never been written. So through them, hopefully, in some way these poems will help others with similar but very personal and individual journeys.

A very big thank you goes to all the children and all the families who have let me use their drawings; they are a privilege to use and add something extra to this book.

The rest of the artwork in this book was carefully drawn and so beautifully painted by a very talented artist called Steve Simpson. His sensitivity and artistic ability has captured these visions so brilliantly. Steve continues to draw and paint for others and himself and his contributions to this book are hugely appreciated. He has made these poems come alive and his obvious talent shines through his work. To contact Steve email theartofsimpson@yahoo.co.uk.

A very lovely lady who has encouraged me throughout, and without her this book would not have been published, is the author of the foreword, Bridget Turner. Bridget is the director of care for CHASE Children's Hospice Service who has given so much to so many. I thank her for the confidence she has given to me, and the special words she has chosen to write in this book.

The staff at CHASE Children's Hospice Service have all shown me support and work hard as a team to support every family that comes through the doors. I thank them for being them.

Many thanks goes to Max Clifford who has so generously sponsored the printing of this book. He is a very valued friend of CHASE and we are very grateful for everything that he does.

My very favourite friends - they know who they are - have listened to me reading out and asking for opinions on poems, rhymes and stories on a regular basis! I thank them for being there with their support and encouragement and hope that I have not bored them too much!

To Noble Wilson, a trustee of CHASE for writing such a brilliant chapter for this book, that describes how "Christopher's" began. I thank him for his time and his quickness in completing this for me.

I would also like to thank Pauline and Stephen Law for their very precious and special story of "Julia" their teenage daughter who died in March 2003. I know that she continues to be an inspiration to many people. I hope that this book will also be a tribute to her, her family, and her large circle of friends

Then finally, an acknowledgement for Christopher More-Molyneux, who "Christopher's" is named after. A big thank you to his family and very lovely parents Michael and Sarah, for their special contributions with Christopher's own chapter. This is a privilege to include in my book.

So through Christopher, through these families, staff and friends, I thank them for helping me to write "When Caterpillars Fly".

A new Millennium should be a new start
A time to reflect on the wrong things we have done
A time to stop wars and poverty
A time to stop sadness
An end to child abuse
Everyone should be friends
Kind to each other
Everyone should resolve to try harder
So this world can be a better place
For everyone to work and play in
Everyone should be safe

Wherever they are

Written by Julia Law at the age of 9

"Do you believe in fairies?
..If you believe, clap your hands!"

J. M. Barrie (1860-1937)